FAMOUS TRAINS OF THE 20TH CENTURY

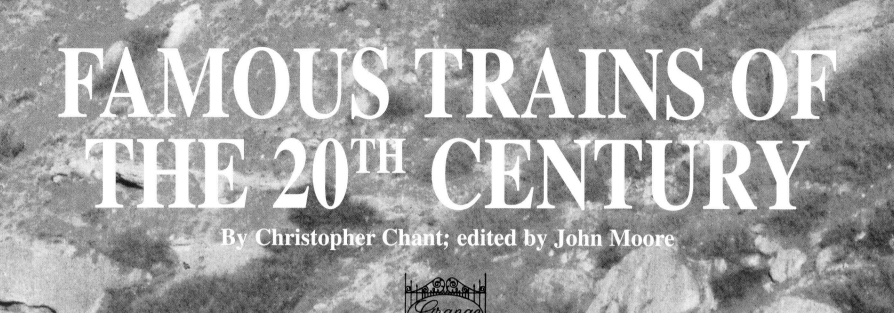

FAMOUS TRAINS OF THE 20TH CENTURY

By Christopher Chant; edited by John Moore

Grange
BOOKS

Published in 2002 by
Grange Books
An imprint of Grange Books Plc
The Grange
Kingsnorth Industrial Estate
Hoo, nr Rochester
Kent ME3 9ND
www.grangebooks.co.uk

ISBN 1 84013 461 5

Printed in Hong Kong

TITLE PAGES: *The east-bound* San
Francisco Zephyr *climbs Echo Canyon,
Utah, behind F40PH locomotives 319
and 354.*

RIGHT: *Eurostar 3015/3016 of the
London–Paris service passing the old
Folkestone Racecourse, England.*

PAGE 5: *Castle-class 4-6-0 7001 Sir James
Milne near Westerleigh, England with the
Cornishman.*

Famous Trains of the 20th Century

Although much, indeed the majority of the work undertaken by railroads and railways is of the workaday type, in tasks as humdrum as the movement of freight and commuter passengers, there have always been a number of passenger services that have nonetheless managed to capture the imagination. This is possibly due to the great expanses of terrain these services occasionally cover, the romantic nature (real or supposed) of the cities they link, or simply because of the phenomenal beauty or ruggedness of the country through which they pass. These services came into existence and became famous comparatively soon after the introduction of the steam locomotive and the longer journeys that were made possible for larger numbers of passengers, and the fact that they caught the attention was signalled by the romance of the names which were given them. Some of these named services have disappeared for compelling political or economic reasons, the latter generally involving the emergence, during the last quarter of a century, of air transport as the primary means of mass transportation over longer distances; but others have adapted and survived to become listed as some of the most famous services of the 20th century.

In North America, only one transcontinental train journey for passengers is still operating across Canada, over a distance of 2,776 miles (4467km). This route connects Toronto toward the eastern side of the country with Vancouver on its western seaboard, and is the so-called Canadian National Route operated by the VIA Rail Corporation. The service operates three times per week as the *Canadian*, a name taken over from Canadian Pacific, the operator which inaugurated the route during 1954 using the first streamlined sleeper train to run in Canada. The *Canadian* takes three days and nights to cover the route, which is a combination of touring and point-to-point transport. Thus the *Canadian* includes cheaper accommodation for the passengers using the service for point-to-point transport, and that which is more expensive for the passengers taking the train for its touring aspect and therefore prepared to pay a premium for more comfort and superbly refurbished public cars, which include club, dining and observation units.

Although the railroad services across Canada once started in Montreal, today's starting point is Toronto, and the route proceeds via Capreol (near Sudbury, Ontario), Sioux Lookout, the Manitoba lake district and Winnipeg, which lies 1,217 miles (1958km) distant from Toronto. At Winnipeg the *Canadian* halts for one hour, and then continues west across the rolling grain-farming plain of central Canada to Saskatoon, Saskatchewan and Edmonton in Alberta. Leaving the plains, the *Canadian* then climbs into the Rocky Mountains. The first stop in the mountains is Jasper, where the *Canadian* rests for 70 minutes while some of the cars are diverted to the *Skeena*, another classic Canadian service that connects Edmonton with the western seaboard at Prince Rupert. Now smaller, the *Canadian* pushes on through the Rockies, traversing the Yellow Head Pass before dropping down to Kamloops. From here it embarks on the final stage of its route, travelling alongside the Fraser river, which carried the tracks of the Canadian Pacific Railway on its other bank, down to the terminus at Vancouver on the third morning from the departure of the service from Toronto. The essentially non-stop nature of the service means, inevitably, that some of the finest scenery is passed unseen in the night, but the scheduling of the service ensures that the best views in the Rocky Mountains are seen in daylight.

It is worth noting that Canada could

once offer three transcontinental routes, but experience soon revealed that there was inadequate traffic to support all three. One of the routes closed, leaving just two after the establishment of Canadian National out of the previous Grand Trunk, Canadian Northern and Grand Trunk Western privately owned systems. Up to 1967 there were four transcontinental services every day from the eastern terminus at Montreal. Competition from jet-powered aircraft was certainly a major factor in the scaling-down of these services, but another and indeed more damaging factor was the inauguration of the Trans-Canada Highway in 1968. The loss of traffic meant that the service was very soon scaled down to one train three times per week, but this schedule now seems secure through the combination of steady point-to-point traffic and its inclusion in the plans of a growing number of tourists, especially from Germany, the U.K. and the U.S.A.

Farther to the south, in the United States, James J. Hill was appreciated then as now to be a giant of the railroad business. By 1901 Hill controlled three American railroads serving what was then little more than the wilderness of the Pacific North-West region. These railroads

were the Great Northern, the Northern Pacific and the Burlington, which were collectively known as the 'Hill Railroads'. Hill's single most celebrated train was the *Oriental Limited*, which connected Chicago, Illinois and the Twin Cities of Minneapolis and St. Paul, Minnesota with Seattle, Washington, where connection could be made with steam ships also run by Hill to link the Pacific North-West with

OPPOSITE: The majestic mountains of Canada create scenery of phenomenal ruggedness and beauty to delight the eye of the railroad passengers.

BELOW: Royal Hudson-class 4-6-4 locomotive 2860 British Columbia, running on British Columbia Railway's North Vancouver to Squamish excursion, above the strait of Georgia, in the late 1970s.

Japan and China. During 1929, after the trans-Pacific route had faded from importance, the railroad created a magnificent transcontinental service that it named in honour of Hill as the *Empire Builder*.

Although the Great Northern and Northern Pacific, which also served Seattle from the Twin Cities, operated separately from each other, the creation during 1971 of the semi-nationalized Amtrak as a federal corporation resulted in the decision that only the Great Northern route, closer to the U.S. border with Canada, should carry a prestigious passenger train while the more southerly Northern Pacific concentrated on freight services. The prestige service is still called *Empire Builder*, and is probably the best transcontinental railroad service in the U.S.A. and, since 1980, has been able to boast an operation with most modern 'superliner' equipment including day cars, a dining car, a sightseeing lounge car and sleeping cars, all 17ft (5.2m) above track level for the best possible fields of view consonant with safe operation.

The first 427 miles (687km) of the route, from Chicago to St. Paul, are over the Burlington Railroad's tracks, but from St. Paul over the distance of 1,795 miles (2888km) to Seattle, the Great Northern's tracks are used, and the whole journey is 2,222 miles (3575km). The eastern terminus is the Union Station in Chicago, and from here the route proceeds basically west via Milwaukee, along the Mississippi river virtually to the Twin Cities, and then the open plains west of Minneapolis. During its

OPPOSITE: *From the comfort of the domed observation cars, passengers could enjoy the spectacular scenery of the Rockies, clearly visible from the* Canadian.

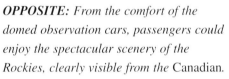

ABOVE: *Special carriages on Canadian trans-continental trains enabled passengers to enjoy to the full the superb panorama.*

ABOVE RIGHT: *The staff of the Canadian National Railways' ticket office, Vancouver, British Columbia.*

RIGHT: *A telegraphy operator at his job, 1942.*

first night on the tracks, the service halts at Fargo, the town where the Wells Fargo (and precursor of the current American Express) was established, and during the morning of the following day passes Rugby, where an obelisk outside the depot indicates the geographical centre of North America. The *Empire Builder* continues through the plains, in the process passing Glasgow and Havre, to reach Browning, Montana and the start of the climb to and passage over the Rocky Mountains. As the train ascends the eastern side of the mountains, passengers can see to their right the 8,000-ft (2440-m) Triple Peak Divide mountain, whose melting snows in the spring supply water for streams and then a river that finally end in three oceans, namely the Atlantic, Pacific and Arctic. The *Empire Builder* advances

Boston Line, and covers the stretch between Springfield and New Haven on the tracks of the Springfield branch of the North-East Corridor, and then follows the main route of Amtrak's most busy Corridor route the rest of the way to Washington. There can be little doubt, however, that the most interesting section of the entire journey is the portion over the New England Central section, and here the *Vermonter* serves Amherst in Massachusetts and the towns of Brattleboro, Bellows Falls, Windsor, White River Junction, Randolph, Montpelier, Waterbury, Essex Junction and St. Albans in Vermont. During the summer and early autumn, the *Vermonter* shares Bellows Falls depot with the privately operated Green Mountain passenger service carrying tourists on a round trip to Chester, Vermont.

The northbound service departs Washington early in the morning and reaches St. Albans during the evening, while the southbound service reverses this schedule, reaching Washington at about the time its counterpart arrives in St. Albans.

The Western Railroad of Massachusetts was established as a pioneering mountain railroad, and in its original form as completed in the early 1840s departed from Boston, Massachusetts to pass over the Berkshire Hills before connecting with the Erie Canal at Albany, New York. The nature of the route, with a number of fairly long and steep gradients, required the use of powerful steam locomotives. During 1867 the Western Railroad merged with the Boston & Worcester Railroad to form the Boston & Albany Railroad, and in 1900 the

majestically through the magnificent Glacier National Park before crossing the Continental Divide at Marias Pass at an altitude of 5,236ft (1596m), the lowest pass of any railroad route through the Rocky Mountains. From here the *Empire Builder* travels through a country of massed mountains and rivers to Spokane, Washington, and here the portion of the train destined for Portland, Oregon is separated before the rump of the service continues over the final stretch of its journey toward Seattle by means of the Cascade Tunnel, which is 7.75 miles (12.5km) in length and was opened in 1929 as the longest tunnel of the Western hemisphere.

On the other side of the U.S.A., the state of Vermont is regarded as possibly one of the prettiest regions of the country, bordered on its east and west by the states of New Hampshire and New York respectively, and celebrated for its dairy farms, maple syrup and skiing. After the 1995 cancellation of the *Montrealer* as the night service connecting Washington D.C. and Montreal, Canada, Amtrak started a daylight service between Washington and St. Albans, Vermont. Appropriately named the *Vermonter*, the train is operated with the aid of state resources, and is one of the most popular operations in the north-eastern part of the U.S.A. The service includes a distinctive baggage car carrying the name of

the train, and the *Vermonter* also stops at rural towns in Massachusetts, New Hampshire and Vermont which, in the absence of the *Vermonter*, would lack any form of public transport.

Between St. Albans and Palmer, Massachusetts, the *Vermonter* runs over the tracks of the New England Central, a short railroad run by RailTex, a major Texas-based operator of short railroad routes. The New England Central began services during February 1995, only a few months before the inauguration of the *Vermonter*, on tracks once controlled by the Canadian National by means of its Central Vermont subsidiary. South of Palmer, the *Vermonter* reaches Springfield over the tracks of Conrail's

OPPOSITE: *Amtraks's Chicago-Pacific Coast*
North Coast Hiawatha.

ABOVE: *Chicago, Milwaukee, St. Paul & Pacific
4-4-2, on train No. 21,* Chippewa, *near Deerfield,
Illinois, with five cars going at top speed of 80mph
(129km/h), 18 September 1939.*

ABOVE RIGHT: *Chicago, Milwaukee, St. Paul &
Pacific 4-6-4, leaving Milwaukee, Wisconsin with
train No.101,* Afternoon Hiawatha, *with 13 cars
and a top speed of 61mph (100km/h). The Hiawatha
expresses were the fastest scheduled steam trains
ever to run.*

RIGHT: *Amtrak's express* North Coast Hiawatha,
*with vista-dome cars in evidence, rolls through the
Minnesota countryside en route between Chicago
and Seattle.*

LEFT: Milwaukee Road's (Chicago, Milwaukee, St. Paul & Pacific Railroad) Hiawatha *at Columbus, Wisconsin.*

BELOW: Amtrak passenger express train with 'double-decker' cars.

New York Central Railroad leased the route. Since that time, the ownership of the route has changed hands on a number of occasions, but the line is still generally known in New England as the 'B&A'. This section now constitutes the single most attractive element of the route travelled by the Boston segment of Amtrak's *Lake Shore Limited* service. This runs on a daily basis over the distance of 1,017 miles (1636km) connecting Chicago's Union Station and South Station in Boston, and in the segment between Chicago and Rensselaer, New York the *Lake Shore Limited* shares with the New York service.

The eastbound *Lake Shore Limited* departs Rensselaer in the middle of the day for a gentle cruise over the Berkshires, climbing out of the valley of the Hudson river by means of a section of track to the Post Road junction abandoned in the early 1970s after the Penn Central Railroad, which then owned the Boston & Albany, ended the passenger service on the grounds that as all freight traffic made use of the Castleton Cutoff west of Post Road to Selkirk, the passenger line to Albany was no longer required. After Amtrak had revised the passenger service, however, the old track was put back into operation. East of Chatham, New York, the track passes over the New York State Thruway, and soon after this traverses the State Line tunnel, thus named as it is located near the New York and Massachusetts state line. The State Line tunnel has a parallel pair of tunnels, but the northern tunnel was closed down in the latter part of the 1980s. East of Pittsfield,

LEFT: Rolling effortlessly over the Continental Divide at Marias Pass, in the Montana Rockies, Great Northern Railway's famous Empire Builder *speeds westwards toward Seattle and Portland.*

The Empire Builder's *four great domes provide views like these as the streamliner skirts the southern boundary of Glacier National Park for 60 scenic miles.*

BELOW: The eastbound Empire Builder *leaves Belton depot at West Glacier, Montana, heading towards the Rockies and Glacier National Park.*

Massachusetts the track begins the climb up to Washington Summit at an altitude of 1,459ft (445m), the highest point on the old B&A. Near Middlefield, on the slope to the east of the track, there are several of the classic stone bridges built by George Washington Whistler, who originally surveyed and built the line, but which was abandoned in 1912 after the track had been revised onto a line of reduced gradient. The westward service from Boston is generally less attractive to the touring traveller because, except during the longest days of summer, the service passes through the most attractive regions at night.

Covering the 2,000 miles (3219km) between Chicago and Oakland, California, the *California Zephyr* is one of the most popular of the western services now operated by Amtrak, for its progress takes the service through some of the most magnificent scenery in the west between the huge Colorado Front Range and the coast of California. The service also covers the 'big ten' curves west of Denver, Colorado, crosses the Continental Divide by means of the celebrated Moffat Tunnel, passes through the deep Gore and Glenwood Canyons, traverses the Utah Desert and climbs over Soldier Summit to reach Salt Lake City, Utah. The service then moves through the deserts of Nevada, climbs over the Donner Pass in California, and finally travels across the Central valley and along the Carquinez Straits to Oakland.

In overall terms, therefore, the *California Zephyr* can be characterized by the splendour of the country through which

ABOVE LEFT: *Interior view of Amtrak coach No. 34100 on the* Desert Wind *express in Union Station, Ogden, Utah.*

ABOVE: *Amtrak's eastbound* California Zephyr *loads up in Sacramento, California.*

LEFT: *Amtrak's westbound* California Zephyr *leaving Glenwood Springs, Colorado, hauled by an F40PH locomotive.*

BELOW: *Amtrak's eastbound* California Zephyr *leaving Green river, Utah behind a F40PH locomotive.*

RIGHT: *Amtrak's westbound* California Zephyr *travelling through Glenwood Canyon, Colorado.*

LEFT: *Amtrak's eastbound* California Zephyr *heads away from Green river, Utah, with the Roan cliffs in the background. It has three F40PH locomotives, two baggage cars and 12 coaches.*

OPPOSITE: *An Amtrak three-powered unit hauls double-decker cars on an express train.*

it passes for most of its distance, whereas most other classically beautiful routes have only isolated sections of excellence. Among the other highlights of the route covered by the *California Zephyr* are those of the climb from the Great Plains to the heights of the Front Range, where there are apparently endless horizons, and the west slope of Donner Pass as the service crosses the Smart Ridge dividing the Yuba and American river valleys and aligns itself with the American river canton: as the river disappears into this deep split in the earth, the railroad track continues high on the northern side of the ravine along the route laid out in the 1860s by the Central Pacific Railroad. At American, just to the east of Alta, California

the track adheres to the very lip of the canyon some 2,000ft (610m) above the river's swirling waters.

The original *California Zephyr* service was launched in 1949 but was terminated during 1970. The current service covers basically the same route except for the use of the Donner Pass rather than the original Feather river canyon. Amtrak's revived *California Zephyr* service was started in the middle of the 1970s, but it was 1983 before it began to use the Denver & Rio Grande Western Railroad's line over the Front Range.

The 1,389-mile (2235-km) *Coast Starlight* route, which links Seattle and Los Angeles, California, is Amtrak's most

prestigious service on the western seaboard of the U.S.A. The *Coast Starlight* provides first-class accommodation as well as superb country along the full length of the route: as the advertising material has it, the *Coast Starlight* is the 'hottest train with the coolest scenery'. The service crosses several ranges of mountains, including the Cascade and Coast Ranges in Oregon and California respectively, and to the south of San Luis Obispo, California, travelling along the Pacific coast for some distance. At Oakridge to the south of Eugene, Oregon, the *Coast Starlight* starts its climb into the Oregon Cascades. The Southern Pacific Railroad built the Cascade Route during the mid-1920s, when it inaugurated the Natron

Cutoff between Black Butte and Eugene, and this is among the most phenomenal tracks in the west of the U.S.A. A short distance from Oakridge, the tracks pass across a tall trestle structure at Heather among towering evergreen trees, and then climb their twisting way up the mountain through a series of long snowsheds and tunnels. In the region of Cruzatte, the tracks pass from a tunnel into a snowshed, then traverse a tall curved trestle over the Noisy Creek into another snowshed, then enter a long curved tunnel.

The view from the *Coast Starlight* is splendid in the summer, but truly superb in the winter when the trees around the tracks are burdened with pristine white and the

snowsheds really fulfil their task of protecting the tracks from the snowy avalanches. Unfortunately for the traveller, the southbound *Coast Starlight* generally passes over the Cascades at night during the winter months, although the northbound service does not suffer from this disadvantage.

Amtrak does not serve San Francisco directly, but passengers for this metropolis can alight and board a bus service at Emeryville station, or alternatively transfer

to a Cal Train commuter service at San Jose. In Oakland, the *Coast Starlight* runs down the Embarcedero through Jack London Square, where the service halts at Oakland depot. Between the agricultural region of the Salinas valley and San Luis Obispo, the *Coast Starlight* advances over the 14 miles (22.5km) of the steep Cuesta Grade, a section of the railroad that winds through some of the most attractive scenery in California. Further progress takes the *Coast Starlight* through Vandenberg Air

Force Base, and to the north of Santa Barbara the tracks pass over a huge trestle at Gaviota before paralleling several popular beaches. The southern terminus of the service is Los Angeles' Union passenger terminal, one of the United State's last great passenger stations, which was completed only in 1939.

The country to the south of the U.S.A. is Mexico, and here the 1961 inauguration of North America's newest transcontinental railroad opened the way for travellers to see

canyons both deeper and longer than the Grand Canyon in Colorado. Connecting the cities of Los Mochis, on Mexico's western coast, and Chihuahua, the 407-mile (655-km) Chihuahua Pacifico Railway is very successful, and provides the only surface transportation across the Sierra Madre mountains with the aid of 87 tunnels and 36 bridges as well as a triple loop at one stage, so that the tracks do not have too steep a gradient as they gain altitude. The summit of the tracks is 8,209ft (2502m) near the

Divisadero halt, the point at which the Barranca (copper) Canyon splits off from the almost equally incredible Ulrique Canyon.

Schemed toward the end of the 19th century as a freight route linking Texas and Central America with the deep-water ports of Mexico's western coast, the railroad progressed only with extreme difficulty and therefore took some 60 years to complete. There is now a schedule of two daily passenger services in each direction, resulting in what is generally believed to be among the five greatest scenic railroad services in the world, and there are also two daily freight services, one in each direction. The passenger services make an early-morning start to ensure that the best possible views are obtained by the passengers, whose numbers are swelled on one day a week by the attachment, at Sufragio, of the cars of the *Sierra Madre Express*, which are hauled to the junction from Nogales.

Altogether different, and redolent of another railway age, is the 234-mile (376-km) passenger journey by the Ferrocaril Presidente Carlos Antonio Lopez of the Paraguayan system between Asunción and Encarnación. This is the only part of the country's railroad system that carries passengers, and the trains are pulled by steam locomotives burning wood in their fireboxes. It was in 1861 that the first part of the route, linking Asunción and Paruguar, opened for business, and in 1889 the railroad was bought by a British-controlled operation, the Paraguay Central

ABOVE: *Amtrak's* Coast Starlight *leaves Seattle for Los Angeles and runs past the cargo yard, hauled by Nos. 547 and 568 locomotives with two baggage cars and ten coaches.*

LEFT: *The* Rio Grande Zephyr *runs into Glenwood Springs, Colorado on its westbound run to Salt Lake City in Utah, behind EMD E9 locomotives Nos. 5771, 5763 and 5762.*

OPPOSITE: *Amtrak's eastbound* San Francisco Zephyr *emerges from a tunnel and crosses the Weber river in Weber Canyon, Utah.*

Railway. The line reached Encarnación in 1911, and was nationalized in 1961. The line was originally built in the 5ft 6in (1.67m) gauge, but in 1911 was narrowed for full interchangeability with the Argentine national railroad system.

The journey between Asunción and Encarnación takes between 14 and 18 hours, and from Asunción moves south-east through rolling country to Villarica, and from this point the rest of the trip is undertaken through a mixture of flat pampas grassland and marshy areas. At Encarnación the traveller can change onto a service for Argentina, the cars being hauled along the city's main street before being lowered into a ferry for movement, six cars at a time, to Posadas on the Argentine side of the Paraná river. The service between Asunción and Encarnación is operated

twice each week, and is hauled by old British locomotives, generally manufactured by North British of Glasgow or Yorkshire Engineering of Sheffield. There are only nine somewhat primitive passenger cars, the single sleeping car having been withdrawn in 1972 and the single dining car disappeared from service shortly after this.

On the other side of the Atlantic Ocean, and created on altogether smaller geographical and engineering scales, one of the most beautiful railway journeys in the U.K. is the 42-mile (67.5-km) service operated since 1901 between Fort William and Mallaig on the West Highland Line along the rugged west coast of Scotland. Departing from Fort William, virtually in the shadow of Ben Nevis, Britain's highest mountain, the service crosses the River Lochy and then the swing bridge over the Caledonian Canal. The line passes round the northern shore of Loch Eil to reach Locheilside at the western end of the loch. The line then proceeds a short distance

ABOVE: Amtrak's Coast Starlight *hauled by locomotives Nos. 642 and 555 passes the ARGO freight yards as it leaves Seattle for Los Angeles.*

RIGHT: Amtrak's Coast Starlight *to Oakland, Portland and Seattle leaving Los Angeles hauled by locomotives Nos. 569 and 567.*

OPPOSITE: Amtrak's Seattle–Los Angeles Coast Starlight *as it travels alongside the Pacific Ocean.*

along a narrow glen to reach the 21 arches of the celebrated Glenfinnan viaduct and, via this, Glenfinnan. Further progress takes the service to the edge of Loch Eilt. From Lochailort station, a sequence of short tunnels and then another viaduct carries the service across Glen Mamie to reach the Atlantic coast at Loch nan Uamh, and then another sequence of short tunnels ducts the line to Arisaig. Here the line turns north, and at Morar it crosses the River Morar before a final 3-mile (5-km) run to the station at Mallaig, a small port dedicated mainly to fishing.

The enjoyment that could be derived from the journey by the passenger was considerably enhanced by the availability of an observation saloon in which there was a running commentary on the interesting features of the route. These Gresley observation carriages were the last of their type in the U.K. and were also very popular with passengers, despite the fact that their use required additional payment, but they had to be withdrawn when the turntable at Mallaig was dismantled, thereby making it impossible for the railway staff to turn them. During the summer, some of the trains are hauled by steam locomotives.

The name *Flying Scotsman* began to impinge on the consciousness of Britain on the very first day of 1923, for it was on this date that the express service of this name was inaugurated, covering the 404 miles (650km) of the route connecting London and Edinburgh, the capital of Scotland. Express services on this route began in 1862, with a journey time of 10 hours 30 minutes, a figure that has been steadily reduced to a current figure in the order of 4 hours 30 minutes. In the period up to 1935, the *Flying Scotsman* was generally hauled by an 'Atlantic'-type locomotive in the section between King's Cross Station in London and Leeds, where the task was taken over by an 'A3'-class locomotive of the 'Pacific' type as far as Newcastle, where another Pacific-type locomotive took over for the final section to Edinburgh's Waverley Station.

After leaving King's Cross Station, the *Flying Scotsman* passed through nine tunnels and then across the Welwyn viaduct of 40 brick-built arches before steaming via Stevenage, Hitchin, Huntingdon, Peterborough, Grantham and Retford to Doncaster. Further northward progress was by means of Wakefield and Leeds. Here, after the engine had been changed, the train was reversed out of the station before turning north once more to reach Newcastle and another engine change before passage into the border regions around Berwick-on-Tweed. Crossing into Scotland, the line generally parallels the coast for the rest of the distance to Edinburgh.

Throughout its course, the *Flying Scotsman*, later hauled by diesel-engine locomotives and now by electric locomotives, passes through some of the most attractive scenery in the eastern part of England, and also traverses some excellent pieces of civil engineering of the heyday of the Victorian age. These artefacts include numerous bridges, viaducts and tunnels.

LEFT: Wood, not coal, fuels this Paraguayan locomotive.

OPPOSITE
LEFT: British Rail No. 37405 climbs slowly to County March Summit on the West Highland Fort William–Glasgow line, Scotland.

RIGHT: The Mallaig to Fort William service, headed by a Class 37 diesel, passes a lighthouse on the Caledonian Canal.

The London & North Western Railway, known as the *Irish Mail*, was the first service anywhere in the world to be named. The service, covering the 264-mile (425-km) route between London and Holyhead on the island of Anglesey off the north-western coast of Wales, where the ferry to Ireland is boarded, was originally known unofficially as the *Wild Irishman*, and first ran in August 1848. The service departed from Euston Station in London and began its exit from the British capital via the Primrose Hill tunnel and then, some 17 miles (27km) from Euston Station, the Watford tunnel, that was created so that the railway line did not cross the estate of the Earl of Essex. Some 35 miles (56km) farther along the tracks, the *Irish Mail* crossed over the Wolverton viaduct of six arches and then, 10 miles (16km) still farther on, the Kilsby tunnel that is 7,270ft (2216m) long and, at the time of its

completion, the world's longest railway tunnel. Further progress took the *Irish Mail* through Birmingham, Manchester, Crewe and Chester before it reached the north coast of Wales, where the main towns are Rhyl and Colwyn. Shortly after Colwyn, the line passes underground once more, in this instance to emerge on the other side of the headland known as Penmaen Mawr. In this region there was inadequate space between the mountain and the shore for the line, and in some places, as a result, the stone of the mountain had to be blasted, and in others large sea walls had to be constructed to allow the outward extension of the coastline so that there was room for the tracks to be laid. Covered ways were made to protect the railway line in areas where it was felt that it might be damaged by rocks and smaller stones falling from the steep side of the mountain. The work of pushing the line forward was severely hampered when,

during October 1846, the combination of a gale and a spring tide swept away a considerable part of the progress that had been made on the western side of the headland, and it was at this stage that the engineers decided that the better solution, then adopted, was an open viaduct to take the tracks into Bangor.

A fact worthy of recognition with regard to the line between London and Holyhead was the installation during 1860 of the world's first water troughs: laid between the two rails just to the east of Bangor, these troughs allowed the train to collect water as it proceeded, without the need for a halt on the section between Chester and Holyhead. The *Irish Mail* then reached the Menai Strait between the mainland of Wales and the island of Anglesey. Here a classic railway bridge was built under the supervision of Robert Stephenson with a span of 1,100ft (335m)

over the fast currents of the strait. Stephenson initially planned for the bridge to be made of cast iron with intermediate piers, but this plan was vetoed by the Admiralty, which demanded that there should be no obstruction of the strait as a possible menace to shipping. Stephenson considered a number of alternative plans before opting, in March 1845, for the use of tubular wrought-iron beams to create a bridge with 460-ft (140-m) openings and also a roadway, formed of a hollow wrought-iron beam with a diameter of about 20ft (6m). The resulting Britannia Bridge has four spans, two of them 460-ft (140-m) long over the water and the other two 230-ft (70-m) long over the land. The bridge was opened for public use in March 1850, doing away with the previous system in which the railway passengers had been compelled to disembark in Bangor and cross the Menai Strait by coach by means of Telford's suspension bridge, before re-embarking on a train for the final stage of the journey to Holyhead and the ferry to Ireland.

One of the most fascinating railway journeys in England has for long been that represented by the 304 miles (490km) between London and Penzance, the latter located at the south-western corner of the county of Cornwall. The line was inaugurated in August 1859, and at that time the train service halted at virtually every station and the passengers had also to change at Exeter and Plymouth before they arrived at Truro, where they were conveyed by horse-drawn carriage to Falmouth, where they boarded the West Cornwall narrow-gauge railway for the 33-minute culmination of their journey in Penzance. The fastest possible journey time from London to Penzance was 14 hours 50 minutes.

In 1862 the route saw the introduction of the *Flying Dutchman* service, which covered the route between Paddington Station in London and Churston on the Torquay branch of the South Devon Railway at an average of 56mph (90km/h), making feasible a time of 10 hours 20 minutes between London and Penzance. In 1863 the basic line was extended from Truro to Falmouth, removing the need for the horse-powered relay, and by 1867 the broad-gauge track of the Great Western Railway had been extended to Penzance. In 1890 the Great Western Railway introduced the *Cornishman* express service, which did not halt at as many stations and was therefore able to reach Penzance in only 8 hours 42 minutes. After the Great Western Railway had been forced to comply with the standard gauge of the other British railway companies, completing its conversion of the Penzance line in 1892, the *Flying Dutchman* was able to trim 15 minutes off its time, in the process becoming the world's fastest main-line

railway service. During 1896 the *Cornishman* recorded a time of 3 hours 43 minutes during a non-stop service to Exeter, at that time the world's longest non-stop route with a distance of 194 miles (312km), and trimmed the time to Penzance to 7 hours 52 minutes. During July 1904 the new *Cornish Riviera Limited*, running non-stop to Plymouth, reached Penzance in exactly 7 hours, further reductions in the

ABOVE: Gresley A3-class 4472 Flying Scotsman *at Carnforth. The* Flying Scotsman *service was inaugurated on the first day of 1923, and covered the 404 miles (650km) between London and Edinburgh.*

time coming in May 1914 with a figure of 6 hours 30 minutes and in 1927, after the introduction of the 'King'-class locomotives as the most powerful engines in Britain, to 6 hours 25 minutes.

Leaving Paddington Station, the train passes over the Wharncliffe viaduct, which was built in 1838 with eight 69-ft (21-m) spans, and the next notable feature of the journey is the Sounding Arch Bridge built in 1838 and widened in 1891. This bridge is one of Isambard Kingdom Brunel's masterpieces, and has two large but very flat brick-built arches each spanning 128ft (39m), but with a rise of a mere 24ft 3in (7.4m). Another major achievement in engineering terms is the Sonning Cutting, which is some 4 miles (6.5km) long and 60ft (18m) deep: the cutting was made in 1839 and opened in 1840 after considerable construction problems had been overcome. In its early period, a notable feature of the Great Western Railway's line to the south-west of England was the number of one-sided stations created under Brunel's supervision: both platforms were on the same side, but set a short distance apart, and this removed the need for passengers to cross the line (either over the tracks or by a bridge) to change between the up-train and down-train sides typical of other companies' stations. Such stations were built at Reading, Taunton and Exeter, but none now survives.

Located on the border between the counties of Somerset and Devon, the 3,274ft (998m) of the Whiteball Tunnel paved the way toward the flat, fast run

LEFT and BELOW LEFT: The Irish Mail *crosses the fast currents of the Menai Strait between mainland Wales and the island of Anglesey. The Britannia Bridge was built under the supervision of Robert Stephenson, who used tubular wrought-iron beams to create a bridge with four spans, two of them 460ft (140m) long over the water and two 230ft (70m) long over the land.*

BELOW: Throughout its history, the Flying Scotsman *has been hauled by steam engine, diesel engine and electric motive power. Here a Deltic 7 locomotive heads this famous train.*

OPPOSITE

LEFT: HST 43 and 43041 locomotive passing Talacre on the Holyhead–Euston line, nicknamed the Irish Mail.

RIGHT: A 47-class locomotive arrives at Penzance with the Cornishman.

along the coast of the English Channel, characterized by the Kennaway, Phillot, Clerk's, Coryton and Parsons tunnels between Dawlish and Teignmouth, and during 1905 the tunnels were widened so that a double-track arrangement could be introduced. Passing through Newton Abbot and proceeding still farther to the south-west, the line crosses from Devon into Cornwall by means of the Royal Albert Bridge, which is 1,109ft (338m) long and spans the River Tamar. The world's only

chain-link suspension bridge with the strength to support express trains, the Royal Albert Bridge should be regarded as Brunel's civil engineering masterpiece: two tubular main spans, each 450ft (137m) long, are supported by three piers that allow a clearance of at least 100ft (30m) from the water. The central pier, whose footings are anchored in rock 79ft (24m) below the river's high-water level, was constructed by masons working in a pressurized diving bell, and this was the first time such

equipment had been used for civil engineering. The construction of the Royal Albert Bridge took seven years, and was opened in May 1859, just four months before Brunel's death.

Over the 53-mile (85-km) section of the route linking Plymouth and Truro, the line passes over 34 viaducts. These were originally timber units designed by Brunel, but were later rebuilt in brick. Created to span the area's large numbers of deep but narrow valleys leading down into the sea,

the viaducts were made in two standard spans, with a length of 66ft (20m) for use on the Cornwall and Tavistock lines, and 50ft (15m) for use in western Cornwall. The line reached Penzance in March 1852, when it opened to standard-gauge trains, but 15 years later the Great Western Railway's broad gauge reached the town.

Despite the fact that the South Eastern & Chatham Railway and its successor, the Southern Railway, had operated services from Victoria Station in London to Paris,

France, it was May 1929 before this service was dignified with a name to indicate its special role. The name of this prestige service was the *Golden Arrow*, and while the first such trains were intended solely for first-class Pullman passengers and hauled by 'Lord Nelson'-class 4-6-0 steam locomotives, the onset of the depression led to the decision of May 1931 to add second-class accommodation to broaden the service's passenger base and thereby ensure its survival through lean times. In

the period following, the tractive effort was switched to rebuilt examples of the 'Merchant Navy' class of 4-6-2 locomotives, and then from 1951 these were in turn succeeded by 'Britannia'-class 4-6-2 locomotives.

The *Golden Arrow* was one of the first British trains to have a public address system for announcements in French as well as English as befitting an international service. Another notable aspect of the service was the inclusion of the so-called

Trianon cocktail bar, in which the more affluent passengers could ease their thirst. Carrying a Union flag and the French tricolour on the front of the locomotive, the *Golden Arrow* left Victoria Station at 11.00 a.m. every morning, and initially made only moderately fast progress as it navigated the gradients at Grosvenor Bridge, before the Penge tunnel and before Bickley Junction. A further limit on speed at this early stage of the journey was the need to steam through the cutting before Orpington, and

then after Tonbridge came two further gradients before the Sevenoaks tunnel. From this point to the British terminal at Dover Marine the line was essentially level, and this permitted a speed of up to 60mph (96km/h). At Dover Marine, 70 miles (113km) from Victoria Station, the train's carriages were loaded onto the rail-fitted ferry *Canterbury*, which covered the sea distance between Dover and Calais in only 1 hour 15 minutes. At Calais, the carriages were unloaded from the ferry and coupled to a French locomotive, a Pacific-type unit of the Nord railway, for the 184-mile (296-km) run to Paris with the translated name *Flèche d'Or*. The train reached Paris at 5.35 p.m.

The service that was later known as the *Orient Express* was launched during 1883 in eight countries by Georges Nagelmackers, a Belgian mining engineer who had established the Compagnie Internationale des Wagons-Lits to operate sleeping cars on the service linking Paris, Munich and Vienna in 1876. Nagelmackers added the suffix 'et des Grands Express Européens' to the name in 1883 at the time that the service was extended to Bucharest in Romania via Budapest in Hungary, the total journey time being 77 hours outbound and 81 inbound. Passengers wanting to travel to Constantinople (now Istanbul), the capital of the Ottoman Empire, had their journey extended to Giurgiu, where they were ferried across the Danube river to Rustchuk in Bulgaria for the seven-hour railroad trip to the Black Sea port of Varna, where they embarked on a steamer of the Austrian Lloyd line for the final stage to Constantinople. The total time from Paris to Constantinople was 82 hours.

It was appreciated that this route was hardly the most effective, so from August 1888 the service was altered from Budapest onward so that the train now travelled via Belgrade and Nis in Serbia (later Yugoslavia) and then the Dragoman Pass into Bulgaria. Here the service passed through Sofia, the capital, and then proceeded via Tatar Pazardjik to Plovdiv,

ABOVE: The Cornish Riviera Limited, *here photographed in 1953, originally began running in July 1904. It ran non-stop from London to Plymouth to reach Penzance in exactly 7 hours, though further reductions in time occurred later.*

LEFT: The Flying Dutchman *service covered the route between Paddington Station in London and, eventually, Penzance in Cornwall. The service was originally introduced in 1862.*

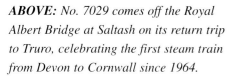

ABOVE: No. 7029 comes off the Royal Albert Bridge at Saltash on its return trip to Truro, celebrating the first steam train from Devon to Cornwall since 1964.

ABOVE RIGHT: An 1859 engraving of the Royal Albert Bridge.

where it moved onto the track of the Oriental Railway for the last leg into Constantinople. The total distance of this service was 1,996 miles (3212km), and this was covered in a little more than 67 hours.

From 1888 the service was considerably upgraded, and after this time the passengers had very comfortable sleeping cars as well as the other standard features of Wagons-Lits luxury, including a dining car serving the best French cuisine. It was in 1891 that the service finally received the name *Orient Express*, by which it is still known, and among the people who enjoyed its attractions were European diplomats, the nobility and at times even royalty.

The *Orient Express* departs from the Gare de l'Est in Paris, and then proceeds up the valley of the Marne river to the Champagne region toward Épernay and Châlons where, at a later date, provision was made for the addition of extra cars coming south from Calais for connections from the U.K. From Châlons the service steamed to Nancy after crossing the Moselle river and passed into Germany at Deutsch-Avricourt, thereafter travelling though Alsace and the Homarting-Arzwiller railroad tunnel that was paralleled by the tunnel for the Marne-Rhine canal. After passing Strassburg (now Strasbourg), the *Orient Express* crossed the Rhine river at Kehl and advanced into Baden-Württemburg. The route now proceeded via Stuttgart, Augsburg and Ulm to Munich, the capital of Bavaria, and thence into Austria-Hungary at Simbach, although the crossing point was soon shifted past Lake Prien to Salzburg. The next halt was Vienna, the capital of the Austro-Hungarian Empire, and from 1894 the service here had a connection with the express service from Ostend in Belgium, passing from Austria into Hungary and then Romania via Bratislava, Budapest, Szged and Timisoara to Bucharest. From the Romanian capital the service crossed the Danube river by means of the Peiterwarden bridge and passed into Serbia at Subotica before an easy sector via Nis to Plovdiv, where passengers to Greece changed. From Plovdiv, the *Orient Express* steamed down

ZURICH ARLBERG STAMBUL
STUTTGART BELGRAD STAMBUL

CIE INTERNATIONALE DES WAGONS-LITS

PULLMAN CAR

LEFT: *The* Orient Express *service, the epitome of luxurious and exotic travel, was launched (though not known by that name) in 1883, and continues to this day.*

OPPOSITE: *In 1929, the prestigious train service operating from Victoria Station, London to Paris was given the name* Golden Arrow, *and the locomotives carried both the Union flag as well as the French tricolour.*

the valley of the Maritza river to enter Greece and pass along the coast of the Aegean Sea to Salonika (now Thessaloniki) and thence the Sirkeci station in Constantinople.

In 1900, the Wagons-Lits company launched a service linking Berlin and Constantinople via Breslau (now Wroclaw), thereby avoiding Vienna, but this experimental operation lasted only two years.

The *Orient Express* was abruptly brought to a halt in 1914 by the outbreak of World War I, both sides then adapting their passenger cars for use as railroad ambulance transports. During 1916, in the middle of World War I, the Germans established the Mitropa company to provide a service between Berlin and Constantinople, and employed requisitioned Wagons-Lits cars for this *Balkan Express* service designed to provide a significant link with their Turkish allies. After the Armistice that ended World War I in November 1918 there were moves to re-establish the *Orient Express* service as rapidly as possible, but the severe disruption of the physical infrastructure

during the war combined with political and economical turbulence after it to make the resumption of *Orient Express* services possible only in 1921. (Interestingly enough, this document was signed in the Wagons-Lits Dining Car No. 2419, which was later destroyed at Hitler's insistence by SS troops during 1944.) In 1923, as a result of the Franco-Belgian occupation of the Rheinland after Germany defaulted on the payment of its war reparations, the service was diverted via Zürich in Switzerland and the 6.5-mile (10.5-km) Arlberg tunnel, which had been completed in 1884, and this revision soon became permanent.

Other notable European services of the period included the Swiss *Arlberg-Vienna Express*, renamed the *Arlberg-Orient Express* in 1932, which ran from Vienna to Budapest via Hagyeshalom, and to Bucharest via Sighisoara, a sleeper service between Paris and Athens that ran twice a week, and a service between Paris and Istanbul that ran three times a week.

Disrupted again by World War II, even though there was for a time a more limited alternative operation between Zürich and

ABOVE LEFT: *The Swiss main line was electrified in 1906, the same year the Wagons-Lits company started the* Simplon Express *service as a major link connecting Paris and Lausanne in Switzerland.*

LEFT: *The Brig portal of the Simplon Tunnel which was the longest tunnel in Europe up to 1991.*

ABOVE, TOP and OPPOSITE: *A pre-production prototype of a TVG (Train Grande Vitesse) at the Gare de Lyon, Paris during trials on existing track in 1979.*

Istanbul, the *Orient Express* was resumed in 1947 with ordinary coaches as well as one or two sleepers and occasionally a dining car. The section between Budapest and Belgrade was terminated in 1963 when the *Tauern-Orient* sleeper service was inaugurated from Ostend to Athens, using the Tauern tunnel that had been completed in 1909. The service was withdrawn in 1976.

Today Wagons-Lits Austria still provides the staff for the sleeper service connecting Vienna and Paris, while a dining car of the Hungarian Railways provides *haute cuisine* on the route between Budapest and Salzburg, and Romanian railways operates the sleeper service between Budapest and Bucharest.

In 1906 the Wagons-Lits company started the *Simplon Express* service as a major link connecting Paris and Lausanne in Switzerland. The route used the recently opened Simplon Tunnel, which was the longest such tunnel in Europe up to 1991, and from Lausanne served Milan and Venice in Italy with the port city of Trieste, at that time part of Austria-Hungary, as its south-eastern terminus. The Viennese authorities would not allow any eastward extension of the service, however, and this meant that the *Simplon Express* covered a route shorter than had originally been planned.

After World War I, the Allied governments involved in the creation of the Treaty of Versailles (signalling an end to Germany's involvement in World War I) created the political framework for the

Simplon-Orient Express. They asked the Wagons-Lits company to run the route, which was expressly designed to provide a link between Western Europe and Romania and Yugoslavia, both recently liberated from occupation, as well as Greece. The new service avoided Austria and Hungary, now separate countries, as well as Germany, which was also forced to allow the resumption of the *Orient Express* service through its territory.

The start of the *Simplon Express* was later moved farther north to Calais on the southern coast of the English Channel, and the connection between the Calais Maritime station and the Gare de Lyon in Paris was provided by the route that had been opened in 1870. From Paris the *Simplon Express* followed the Seine river valley to the Laroche-Migennes point at which a fresh locomotive replaced the original unit, after which there was an easy gradient up to the Blaizy-Bas summit and then a descent to Dijon, the capital of the Burgundy region. Here the route altered to the east, the line climbing from an altitude of 950ft (290m) at Mouchard to 2,955ft (900m) at the entrance to the Mont d'Or tunnel, which opened in 1915 and passes through the Jura mountains to Vallorbe in Switzerland. Before the completion of the tunnel, the *Simplon-Orient Express* was routed through Pontarlier to Vallorbe.

After crossing the Orbe river, the train joined the Swiss main line, which had been electrified in 1906, on the section between Neuchâtel and Lausanne, and then continued along the shore of Lake Geneva through Montreux before following the Rhine valley to Brig at the mouth of the Simplon Tunnel. The line emerged from the tunnel at Iselle in northern Italy, and from this point the Swiss-operated line dropped some 1,180ft (360m) over a distance of 17 miles (28km) through the Trasquera tunnel, Iselle station, the Varzo Spiral Tunnel, five smaller tunnels and the larger Preglia tunnel, before joining the Italian railway system at Domodossola. On the Italian section of its route, the *Simplon-Orient Express* passed Lake Maggiore, and followed the flat line, completed during 1848, from Milan to Venice, passing Lake Garda and Verona. After reversing out from Venice, the train then crossed the causeway to Venice-Mestre, where the line rejoined the coastal main line outside Trieste.

All the passengers had to change at Trieste, but westbound passengers were permitted to sleep in the standing train and catch the connection to Paris during the following morning. From Trieste, the line climbed from sea level to 985ft (300m) at Poggioreale del Carso on the current frontier between Italy and what is now Slovenia but was then part of the Austro-Hungarian empire. The route of the *Simplon-Orient Express* through Laibach (now Ljubljana) and Agram (now Zagreb) continued to Vinkovci-Belgrade and Nis, where it divided: one part went to Constantinople on a thrice-weekly basis and the other to Athens twice weekly. The Constantinople train also had connections to Bucharest, reached via the Vinkovci-Subotica branch line that crossed the Romanian frontier over the Danube river near the Iron Gates. The service provided by the *Simplon-Orient Express* for the entire 2,150 miles (3460km) between Calais and Constantinople took three nights and four days in each direction.

OPPOSITE: Eurostar 3016/3015 approaching the Willesborough level-crossing to the east of Ashford in Kent. The crossing is manually operated and the keeper's hut is just out of view in the left foreground. Note the signboard on the right.

RIGHT: Eurostar at Waterloo Station, London. The Eurostar London–Paris (via the Channel Tunnel) high-speed service moved swiftly from the date of its inception in 1987 to its service debut in 1994. Because of the Channel Tunnel restrictions, it has only two power cars, one at the front of the train and one at the rear.

The service's celebrated blue-and-gold sleeping cars, which were of all-steel construction, first appeared in 1926, four years after their debut on the *Train Bleu*, which was the prestige service linking Calais and San Remo via Nice. By 1929 the *Simplon-Orient Express* was able to offer a daily service from Paris to Istanbul, and this service included a dining car and sleeping cars. During 1930 the *Simplon-Orient Express* became the main prop of the Wagons-Lits company's *Taurus Express*, an even longer route that linked London with Cairo, the capital of Egypt.

The *Simplon-Orient Express* was somewhat revised in 1932, when Ostend-Orient, Amsterdam-Orient, Berlin-Orient, Prague-Orient, Vienna-Orient and Paris-Orient or Arlberg-Orient sleeping cars started to join the service at Belgrade on different days. This provided three daily Istanbul sleepers and two services daily (four from Thessaloniki) to Athens. In overall terms, the *Simplon-Orient Express* can be regarded as a highly romantic (or perhaps romanticized) service whose advertising consciously played not only on the luxury of the operation but also on the 'mystery' of what had until the end of World War I been the Ottoman Empire that had long entranced the thoughts of many Europeans. The service was a popular medium for any number of the Balkan nobility, and King Boris liked to drive the engine of the *Simplon-Orient Express* in Bulgaria. The Wagons-Lits company maintained reserves of block ice, coal and rolling stock all along the route, and this

permitted the maintenance not only of an almost notorious level of luxury and elegance on board, but also (and somewhat more prosaically) a considerable reliability of service in regions little noted at the time for their technical skills. Another feature of the service in the summer months was a shower in the baggage car. The Wagons-Lits company also provided daily dining cars for the Lausanne-Trieste-Svilengrad, Nis-Thessaloniki and Amfiklia-Athens sections of the route and it offshoots, and a kitchen van for the Uzunköprü-Istanbul section.

The outbreak of World War II in 1939 did not at first stop the travels of the *Simplon-Orient Express*, which was eventually brought to a temporary halt only in 1942, and individual sleeping cars with neutral Turkish staff served most of the overnight sectors. The *Simplon-Orient Express* resumed services to Istanbul during January 1946, and in 1949 added a branch service to Athens. The service in the period after World War II had lost much of its pre-war glamour, and this was exemplified by the fact that dining cars gradually became a rarity. The *Simplon-Orient Express* came to an end in 1962, and the last sleeping car service between Paris and Istanbul was operated in May 1977.

At the technical level of modern railroad operations, the 626-mile (1008-km) service between London and Berne, the capital of Switzerland, is one of the most fascinating examples that can be found. The service begins in London's Waterloo Station at the terminal specially built for the so-called *Eurostar* trains, which operate

regular services via the Channel Tunnel to northern European termini at Brussels and Paris. Access to the passenger assembly hall is provided by barriers that automatically scan the service's special tickets: if the ticket is accepted, the barrier's gate opens to allow the passenger through to the security examination area. Every passenger with a first-class ticket is welcomed onto the train by a steward, one of whom waits by the door to each coach, and help can be provided for other passengers.

The design of the *Eurostar* train was undertaken on a collaborative international basis, and the group responsible for the design process based its work on the principles validated in the French TGV (*Trains Grande Vitesse*), but numerous changes were necessary to optimize the design for the new service: factors that had to be borne in mind included the need for the train to operate in the U.K.'s much more restricted loading gauge; the fact that the electrical supply was to come from three different systems, including current collection via a third rail in the U.K.; that there were to be four signalling systems; and that notably demanding safety standards were required for operation through the Channel Tunnel. The design of the train's exterior was British with a central driving position and one window in the front of the cab. The design of the train's interior was a joint Franco-Belgian undertaking, and the success of this team is more than amply suggested by the fact that the *Eurostar* has more usable volume than the TGV despite being smaller in its overall

ABOVE and OPPOSITE LEFT: *Food and beverages are served in the TVG dining areas where passenger comfort is of the utmost importance.*

OPPOSITE RIGHT: *First-class passengers on* Eurostar*'s service from Waterloo to Paris.*

dimensions. At the technical level, especially in the mechanical and electrical aspects of the vehicle, the design team had a number of problems to solve and apparent conflicts to resolve. An instance of the type of problem to be overcome can be found in the particular safety requirements imposed on trains using the Channel Tunnel. It is necessary that passengers can be moved from one end of the train to the other, and this fact made it impossible for additional power units to be used in the middle of the 20-vehicle train: the *Eurostar* train therefore has just two power cars, located at the front and rear of the train, with additional powered bogies under the first and last passenger coach to compensate in part for the loss of the power that two equivalent TGV sets would have provided. Other features that had to be borne in mind

were the need to reduce the overall size of the bogies; the need to provide a taller pantograph to touch the high overhead contact line in the Channel Tunnel; the need to create steps that would automatically adjust to the different heights of the platforms in three countries; and the need to provide all the complicated signalling equipment that was required.

Despite the complexity of the project and the inherent difficulty of co-ordinating the efforts of a three-nation design and industrial team, the *Eurostar* was rapidly and successfully taken from the date of its inception in 1987 to the date of its service debut in November 1994.

At the end of the 20th century, the U.K. still lacks any dedicated high-speed railroad tracks and, as a result, the *Eurostar* has to operate within the context of the dense and

often considerably slower railroad traffic in the south-east of England. In the south-eastern part of London, where the routes of the capital's railway lines were laid down in the 19th century and are therefore somewhat winding in their disposition, the necessarily slow speed of the *Eurostar* at least allows the passenger to see his surroundings. After it has emerged from the city and the suburbs into the countryside of Kent, the train can accelerate to about 100mph (160km/h), especially on the essentially straight section between Tonbridge and Ashford. A number of *Eurostar* services stop at the specially rebuilt Ashford station, which also caters for local and inter-city trains and thus makes feasible a measure of interchange as well as the boarding of passengers who have arrived by car. Shortly after leaving

Ashford, the train switches from the British Rail track network to that of Eurotunnel and arrives at the Dollands Moor conglomeration of sidings, depots and loading docks for cars and heavy goods vehicles. Here the shoes collecting current from the third rail are lifted and the pantograph is raised.

The Channel Tunnel is 31 miles (50km) in length and as such is the second longest railroad tunnel in the world, as well as the tunnel with the longest underwater section. In the Channel Tunnel and on the TGV lines onto which the train emerges on the French side of the tunnel, French cab signalling is used to pass instructions to the train driver. The maximum speed permitted in the Channel Tunnel is 100mph, and the trip takes only about 20 minutes before the train hurtles out of the tunnel

into France near the huge marshalling yards of the Coquelles terminal. The route to Paris lies through the new exchange station at Fréthun, and soon after this the train is travelling on the high-speed tracks through country that is basically level and therefore allowing the creation of a track possessing only gentle, sweeping curves. On this part of the journey it is generally announced on the train's public-address system that the maximum permitted speed of 186mph (300km/h) has been reached.

Facilities for exiting passengers at the Gare du Nord, where the *Eurostar* service from London terminates, are not good, and passengers needing to get to the Gare de Lyon to connect with the Swiss service need to travel by taxi or métro underground link. The TGV used for the service to Switzerland may be Swiss-owned, but is painted in the same livery as the French trains of the same type. Once embarked on the train, the passenger can quickly appreciate the generally superior nature of the *Eurostar* train he has recently quit, despite the greater height and width of the TGV.

The TGV leaves the Gare de Lyon comparatively slowly, for exactly the same reasons as the *Eurostar*'s progress through the southern part of London. However, in the region near the great marshalling yards at Villeneuve St.-Georges, the TGV is passing into a less congested region and can begin to reveal its true performance, especially when, at Lieusaint, it joins the Ligne à Grande Vitesse, generally newly built and optimized for the TGV to operate

at its maximum speed. The track in question is the Sud-Est LGV stretching to Lyons, Valence and, ultimately, Marseilles. The service to Berne and Lausanne uses this line only as far as Passilly, from where there is a short link to the older main line at Aisy. From Aisy to Dijon the track's alignment is good enough to allow the train to maintain a high speed until it is time to decelerate for the approach to Dijon's main station. The fastest services take a mere 99 minutes to complete the 196-mile (315-km) distance from Paris to Dijon.

After departing from Dijon, the TGV veers from the Salines river valley and starts to climb toward the mountains, initially with good views to the right although, as the train climbs ever higher, the views become more restricted as a result of the defiles through

which the train progresses. The train emerges from its climb to reach the plateau town of Frasne, where there is a rail junction. From here the main line runs straight ahead to Vallorbe, a small Swiss town just over the border, and then starts its descent with pleasant views across villages and farmland until its reaches Lake Geneva (Lac Leman) at Lausanne. The other line from Frasne heads off to the left and winds across comparatively flat land until it nears the mountain barrier of the Montagne du Lermont. The track follows a narrow defile through the mountains that is guarded by the town of Pontarlier, with its impressive castles high on the hillsides above the line of the rail and road tracks as these close on the Swiss frontier.

The first village the train approaches on

ABOVE and RIGHT: *Earlier examples of the French railway's TGV (Trains Grande Vitesse) locomotives which had the enormous advantage of running, right from the start, on specially built high-speed track.*

OPPOSITE: *TGV No. 23122 (unit 61) at the Gare de Lyon, Paris.*

Swiss soil is Les Verrières, and slightly farther on St.-Sulpice and Fleurier can be seen below and to the right in the Val de Travers. The railroad tracks carry the train past lovely scenery until a dramatic change brings panoramic views across Lake Neuchâtel. The town of Neuchâtel, again guarded by a castle, is old and lies on the important main line of communication between Basle at one end and Lausanne and Geneva at the other. Neuchâtel's station handles the traffic of the Swiss federal railways and, to a more limited extent, that of the Berne-Lötschberg-Simplon Railway, and it is on the tracks of the latter that the TGV now runs across the generally level and fertile broad plateau to Berne, where the service terminates in the curving and rather gloomy station, well situated near the centre of this small capital city after a run of 4 hours 32 minutes. The timing and speed of the combined *Eurostar* and TGV service between London and Berne are such that the passenger can board the train in London at 9.53 a.m., arrive in Paris at 2.08 p.m. (Central European Time), depart from Paris at 3.50 p.m. and arrive in Berne at 8.22 p.m.

In the northern part of Africa, the service on the main line connecting Casablanca and Gabès carries its passengers right along the south-west coast of the Mediterranean through North Africa between the cities of Casablanca in Morocco and Gabès in Tunisia, a distance of some 1,105 miles (1778km) in all on a line whose construction was started in 1915. A French possession from 1840,

Algeria was treated as a *département* of the metropolitan state, and its Société Nationale des Transports Ferroviaires was built and operated to the French standard as an essentially coastal network to provide communication along the coast of the three French possessions in North Africa. Constructed as a standard-gauge operation, the rail service was generally efficient and reliable in the period up to the outbreak of World War II, but then began to decline during this war and the troubled period following it as France sought to restore its position but faced growing demands for independence from Morocco, Algeria and Tunis, which gained their objectives in 1956, 1962 and 1962 respectively.

Neither the Moroccan nor the Algerian railroads appear to be proud of their

operations, and this is reflected in the essentially run-down nature of their services. Across Morocco from Fez to the Algerian border, the compartments are awash with the bodies of passengers seeking to rest on uncomfortable wooden seats. The border is reached at Oujda, which is a dull but not dismal town characterized by wide streets and solid housing of the European pattern. The initial stages of the passage through Algeria offer a number of odd aspects, including the sight of rusted train wrecks alongside the line before Oran, then an almost Moorish-Spanish style is apparent in Tlemcen, while Sidi-bel-Abbès is wholly redolent of the French Foreign Legion. Even a brief look at Oran reveals the fact that the building of most North African appearance in the city is

the railroad station, where it is claimed that the easiest method of securing a corner seat is to board the train and start a rumour that the train for the service in question is in fact just arriving at another platform.

As in many industrial countries, the railway route into the capital, in this instance from Oran to Algiers, is not a pretty sight as the track penetrates a seedy mass of industrial areas on its way toward the station nearer the centre of the city. Between Algiers and Constantine there are genuinely stunning rock formations and a deep ravine crossed by a slender bridge. The next main station is Annaba, and the service that resumes from this city is one of the most interesting in the world for its awfulness, for it comprises third-class coaches in which a not inconsiderable

number of compartments lack both seats and windows. The next major arrival is at Souk Ahras, the border town some 10 miles (16km) from the Tunisian frontier.

In Tunisia things change dramatically and, fortunately for the traveller, for the better. The train is moderately clean and in much better condition than its Algerian counterpart. On the way to Tunis, customs officers check the baggage of passengers by merely turning it upside down. The 118 miles (190km) between the border and the capital are of narrow metre-gauge track, and this explains why the passengers have had to change trains. In the south of the country, at Sfax, the traveller has to change trains once more. The connection to Gabès is poor, however, and the trains that eventually arrive seem as reluctant as the

traveller is eager to reach the end of the line after the trip from Casablanca.

Organized tourism up the River Nile is now more than 125 years old. The Thomas Cook & Son company, in the form of the son John rather than the father Thomas, began to operate tourist river steamers on the Nile from about the middle of the 1870s. The steamer operation was based in Cairo, Egypt's capital city that was linked with the country's main port of Alexandria by the Middle East's first railroad, constructed in 1855. This link included a bridge over the Nile outside Cairo that is also used by the service extending up the Nile to Aswan. Operating from the Cairo Main station, this service was inaugurated as the *Star of Egypt* by the Wagons-Lits company, which marked its silver jubilee in 1898 by expanding simultaneously into Russia and Egypt.

In Egypt, the company's cars were painted white to reflect heat and also had double roofs to help prevent its ingress, and the dining cars, built by Ringhoffer of the Austro-Hungarian empire, featured a type of primitive air-conditioning in which blocks of ice cooled the air circulating between the skins of the roof. The Wagons-Lits company, which was the great rival to Thomas Cook that it managed to buy in 1928 but lost once more during World War II, inaugurated the initial service between Cairo and Luxor in 1898 with a high-class arrangement that included dining and sleeping cars. To a time at least as late as 1908 the lines extending up the Nile to Aswan were of the narrow-gauge type, and

LEFT: The Union Limited, *connecting Cape Town and Pretoria was renamed the* Blue Train *in 1939 and was painted in a blue-and-cream livery. The train was later hauled by an electric-powered locomotive, with blue-and-gold livery, as seen on this* Blue Train *near Fountains, Pretoria in the mid-1970s.*

OPPOSITE: Spectacular scenery and luxurious travel conditions have delighted passengers on South Africa's Blue Train *for many decades.*

in this year the classic night train left Cairo on Mondays, Wednesdays and Saturdays, returning from Luxor on Tuesdays, Thursdays and Sundays. It was in the same year that the Luxor service was extended to Aswan, a 597-mile (960-km) journey. The line leaves Cairo, crosses the Nile on the Alexandria line bridge and then turns south along the Nile's left (west) bank through Asyût. The line recrosses the Nile at Nag 'Hamâdi, and thereafter follows the right (east) bank of the river to Luxor and Aswan.

In 1906, from the estate of the late George Mortimer Pullman, Lord Dalziel bought the British section of the Pullman operation as well as the exclusive right to the name Pullman on railroad cars

in 1903. This service was run by the Cape Government Railway and the Central South African Railway. Then in 1910, when the Union of South Africa was established, all of the country's independent railroad operators merged to create South African Railways, and the train service between Cape Town and Pretoria was then named the *Union Limited*. Although the train was a luxury one-class express, with a fare somewhat higher than was otherwise standard for the route, it was so popular that in the 1930s more coaches were added for extra capacity, and the smart Pacific-type locomotives hitherto used to haul the train, were replaced by 4-8-2 locomotives.

The twice-weekly train was renamed the *Blue Train* (*Bloutrein* in Afrikaans) during April 1939. This was not, of course, the first time a train service had operated with this name, for the *Train Bleu* service had connected Paris and the Côte d'Azur since the 1920s. This change of name in South Africa coincided with the introduction of new blue-and-cream cars with clerestory roofs, although the locomotives remained unaltered in South African Railways' black livery. The passenger compartments were of the super de-luxe type with dust-proofing and air-conditioning, and the accommodation included blue leather-upholstered seats, loose cushions and writing tables with headed writing paper. At the rear of the train was an observation car. In spite of the railroad track's gauge, the width of these coaches was 10ft (3.05m).

To ensure that there was adequate space

throughout Europe and Egypt. During 1907 Dalziel gave up these rights to Wagons-Lits, of which he was a director. Wagons-Lits began using Pullman cars in about 1925, and the new units for service in Egypt were shipped from England to Alexandria. More Pullman cars were shipped in 1929, when the *Sunshine Express*, an all-Pullman day train from Cairo to Luxor, was begun. New sleeping cars now operated in the night train, named the *Star of Egypt*. At Aswan it continued to El Shallal, above the cataracts and the Aswan Dam, connecting with steamers to Wadi Halfa, in the Sudan, where the Sudanese Railways line to Khartoum avoids a huge bend in the river. When the new Aswan Dam was built, the Aswan terminus

was forced to move to El Sadd el All.

The *Sunshine Express* service ended during 1939, but the sleeping cars were revived after World War II, and the *Star of Egypt* continued until about 1958–59, when the Wagons-Lits operation in Egypt was nationalized. The Egyptians then discovered that they could not really manage without the expertise of the original company, which was then permitted (indeed encouraged) to return, so that a joint company could be created to operate the service. The Hungarian sleeping cars that the Egyptian railroad had bought in the interim were then relegated to use on slow trains, and the modern all-sleeper train, with a lounge car, has rolling stock built in the 1980s by a West German company: the

dining car has been replaced by a supply car, and passengers take their meals in their cabins.

At the present, one train suffices on the service between Cairo and Aswan, as most people prefer either to cruise on the Nile or to fly. The railroad journey between Cairo and Aswan, now an all-sleeper service, takes some 16 hours, which is 30 minutes slower than the equivalent service in 1938.

Much farther to the south on the African continent, the major home of prestige railroad services in South Africa exists. The first luxury train to operate on the 3ft 6in (1.07m) gauge track over the 999-mile (1607-km) route between Cape Town and Pretoria, the country's political but not economic capital, was inaugurated

available for all the various on-board services, which included fully equipped bathrooms, the accommodation was limited to a mere 100 passengers on each journey, and this accommodation had to be booked many months in advance. The train is now hauled by electrically-powered locomotives with blue-and-gold livery between Pretoria and Kimberley and again between Beaufort West and Cape Town, and its schedule is three round trips weekly from October to March and one from April to September. The then President Mandela of the new 'multi-racial' South Africa inaugurated this new version of the *Blue Train* in June 1997. Built from the undercarriage of the original *Blue Train* sets, these two new trains feature only two levels of accommodation (luxury

and de-luxe) as opposed to the previous arrangement of four classes.

The luxury suites differ from the de-luxe accommodation in that they are more spacious and offer larger bathrooms, and whereas de-luxe features a private shower or bath, the luxury suites all have a bath. There is 24-hour butler service, laundry service and two lounge cars, and while all the accommodation has televisions and telephones, the luxury suites also feature little 'extras' in the form of CD players and video recorders. Another attractive and popular feature is the imaging provided by the TV camera positioned on the front of the train, and this provides the passengers with a 'driver's eye-view' of their journey.

The extensive nature of the upgrading

inevitably meant that the capacity of the *Blue Train* had to be reduced, in this instance from a maximum of 107 to just 84. The *Blue Train* no longer serves Johannesburg, but is instead routed through Germiston as it travels between Cape Town and Pretoria, which is also the southern terminus of the classic railroad service to the Victoria Falls in Zimbabwe (originally Rhodesia).

Railroads in what was then the Cape Colony started in 1857, when a pioneering 45-mile (72-km) line was opened from Cape Town to Wellington. In 1873 the first trains completed the 644 miles (1036km) on the route from Cape Town to Kimberley across the Karoo, and as the great imperialist and railroad pioneer Cecil

ABOVE LEFT: *Dining car on the* Trans-Karoo Express, *mid-1970s.*

ABOVE: *In contrast with the packed and noisy commuter trains leaving Cape Town, the long-distance express trains, such as the* Pride of Africa, *offer spacious and pleasant facilities.*

OPPOSITE and Page 48: *A Russia Class P36 heads a passenger train. Russian railways, particularly on the Trans-Siberian route, had strategic objectives as well as carrying passengers.*

Rhodes progressed northward through the southern part of Africa, the railroads were rapidly extended to the north: the 146-mile (235-km) section from Kimberley to De Aar was created in the impressively short period of 20 months between March 1884 and November 1885. This section between Cape South and De Aar is the southern part of the route covered by the *Pride of Africa* service from Cape Town to Victoria Falls via Beaufort West, De Aar, Kimberley, Klerksdorp, Johannesburg, Pretoria, Mafikeng (border), Gaborone, Plumtree (border), Bulawayo and Hwange.

The modernity of the flat-roofed station in Cape Town is perhaps an unlikely spot for the traveller to launch himself on one of the most fascinating and enjoyable railroad journeys anywhere in the word, but it is here that he boards the *Pride of Africa*. Impressive in its bottle-green livery, this train offers, right from the beginning, the promise of a truly memorable experience. At the head of the train, two '6E'-class Bo-Bo electric locomotives, in the livery of South African Railways, sit in a double-heading arrangement to haul the cars over the 440 miles (708km) to Beaufort West, in the course of which the train also climbs from the sea-level altitude of Cape Town to a height of more than 4,000ft (1220m) across the Karoo. Another fact that the traveller can hardly miss is that the spacious accommodation and quiet but friendly welcome onto the service contrast most starkly with the packed and noisy accommodation of the commuter trains linking Cape Town with its suburbs. The

nature of the *Pride of Africa* reflects the desire of Rohan Vos, the service's owner and creator, to offer the very highest of standards, and Vos often appears to see the service on its way as one of the world's most romantic travelling idylls. Rovos Rail is Vos's creation, and in 1986 the company started the restoration of old, derelict railroad cars and of the steam locomotives to haul them. Dating originally from 1919, each sleeping car, bar and lounge car as well as observation car, complemented by still older Victorian and Edwardian dining cars, were sympathetically renovated with nothing of the original 'flavour' lost as modern conveniences were incorporated. The accommodation provided in the sleeping cars comprises suites with double or twin beds, together with private showers and lavatories.

Spread beneath the flat-topped Table Mountain, Cape Town has one of the most dramatic locations on earth. As it begins its journey to the north, the *Pride of Africa* soon emerges from the city and rides the track round the edge of Table Bay before heading inland. In the wine-growing region of Paarl and the Hex river valley, there is a feeling of quiet but determined domestic economy, but an indication of the fact that the traveller is in the southern part of Africa is provided by glimpses of strangeness, such as scrub areas with ostriches clearly at home among sheep and horses. In the last glimmers of daylight, the train arrives at Matjiesfontein. Here there is a one-hour halt, allowing the traveller to investigate this small town in which, late in the 19th

century, Laird Logan set up a small refreshment hotel to restore the equilibrium of travellers on the service of the Cape Government Railways.

As the *Pride of Africa* now continues across the Karoo, most of the passengers gravitate to the observation car to watch the fantastic onset of the South African night, and the setting of the observation car, with its seven pairs of carved roof-supporting pillars and arches, is highly conducive to a feeling of time stretching nostalgically backward into the past. Later, the travellers gather for dinner and finally return to their suites for sleep. Despite the narrow gauge of the South African Railways' track, the ride of the *Pride of Africa* is quite smooth.

At Beaufort West the current changes from DC to AC, and two '7E'-class Co-Co locomotives are attached to haul the train to De Aar. There is now a 146-mile (235-km) stretch of non-electrified line from De Aar to Kimberley, and the electric locomotives are replaced by a pair of '34'-class Co-Co diesel-electric locomotives. During the following day the *Pride of Africa* reaches Kimberley's classic Victorian station. Kimberley, the centre of the South African diamond-mining industry, is located deep in the stark extent of the Karoo. Now with two high-speed '12E'-class Bo-Bo electric locomotives undertaking the traction, the *Pride of Africa* speeds from Kimberley toward Pretoria. The following day the service strikes north through groves of fruit trees, past African townships where flocks of children run down to the tracks smiling and waving, and enters the open country

where in the observation and lounge cars the traveller can embark on his railborne wild-life safari with the first sightings of varied herds of grazing animals.

Crossing into Botswana at Mafikeng, the *Pride of Africa* has the first of seven locomotive changes between Pretoria and the Victoria Falls. The train starts to climb the steep mountains that separate the lush, fertile Hex river valley from the elevated, arid Karoo. The climb of 1,750ft (535m) over a distance of 50 miles (80km) is the single most spectacular section of the journey and also has its highest point at a location just south of Johannesburg, at an altitude of 6,017ft (1834m). There is also a series of four completely straight tunnels in the 10.25-mile (16.5-km) Hex river tunnel system, which ranks it as the fourth largest of its type anywhere in the world.

The last complete day on the train is filled with spectacular views of the African bush. After crossing into Zimbabwe at Plumtree, an afternoon visit is made to Bulawayo, which was once the capital of the Matabele nation and later became the centre of mining in the area. Here the traction effort is assumed by a '15'-class Garratt articulated steam locomotive, and this vast machine hauls the *Pride of Africa* through the night along the 72-mile (116-km) stretch between Gwaai and Dete, one of the world's longest straight stretches. At Dete the service is on the eastern edge of the Hwange National Park, and the halt at Victoria Falls marks the end of the magnificent journey after a distance of some 2,000 miles (3218km).

ABOVE: *The Japanese railway's Shinkansen below Mount Fuji on the Tokyo–Hakata line.*

LEFT: *A Shinkansen, typically mounted on a viaduct to avoid urban congestion.*

OPPOSITE ABOVE and BELOW: *A line-up of four Shinkansen 'bullet trains', while another awaits departure. A Shinkansen service leaves Tokyo every six minutes during peak periods.*

It was during 1858, many thousands of miles to the north, that the first plans for a Trans-Siberian Railway linking Moscow and European Russia with the Pacific coast of Siberia were first promulgated. However, as a result of the Crimean War (1853–56), it was 1875 before an official plan was put forward. There followed a number of other schemes before the year 1891 finally saw the granting of official approval by the Russian government. Moreover, with a speed and determination that appeared unusual in the general lethargy of Russian development during the later part of the 19th century, the Tsarevich Nikolai cut the first sod of grass in Vladivostok. The planned railroad was clearly to be one of the world's greatest and most difficult engineering feats, and was seen by the Russian government as a primary aid in the task of consolidating Russia's hold on Siberia and its Far Eastern reaches on the shores of the Pacific Ocean, in the process improving both the Siberian and overall Russian economies as well as realizing the possibility of being able to exert political pressure on China.

Such was the size of the task faced by the Russians in the construction of the Trans-Siberian Railway that though work began in 1891, it was 1903 before the first through service was operated. This original level of service included a train ferry over Lake Baikal, the deepest lake in the world. During the winter, however, the ice covering the lake soon became too thick to be broken by any current ice breaker, so the train ran over the lake on a specially laid winter section of rail. The land link between Moscow in the west and Vladivostok in the east was finally completed in 1905 when the line round the southern edge of Lake Baikal was finished. Blasted out of the solid rock of the lake's shore, in places 4,000ft (1200m) tall, this 42-mile (68-km) link had no fewer than 38 tunnels which had to be bored, and the steepest gradient was located just to the east of Ulan Ude, where an incline of 1/57.5 had to be climbed.

At first, part of the route was laid across Manchuria (this section of the track is now the Chinese Eastern Railway) to create as direct a route as possible from Chita to Vladivostok via Harbin. This section over Chinese soil was deemed sensible at the time as the fairly flat terrain of Manchuria allowed it to be completed more quickly and more cheaply than would otherwise have been the case. After the Russo-Japanese War (1904–05), which had strained the line to capacity if not actually beyond this point as the Russians sought to rush large numbers of troops and vast quantities of supplies and equipment from European Russia to the Far East, the Russians decided that strategic requirements called for a connection to be constructed from Chita to Vladivostok by means of the Amur river valley and Khabarovsk. Although considerably longer than the direct route across Manchuria, it did ensure that the whole route was at last wholly in Russian territory.

The line, beginning in Moscow and connecting with Vladivostok via Omsk,

Irkutsk (on the shores of Lake Baikal) and Khabarovsk, was created as a single-track route, and by 1913 most of it had been converted to double-track layout. However, it was the 1950s before the complete route was of the double-tracked type. Further upgrading of the Trans-Siberian Railway continued, and by the mid-1970s some three-quarters of the line from the European end had been electrified. One of the most interesting aspects of the Trans-Siberian Railway is its vast number of bridges, large and small, as the line traverses the huge number of valleys that are generally aligned north to south. On the line's western section the bridges include eight with a span of 985ft (300m) or more, including those over the Irtysh, Oh and Yenisei rivers, all of them more than 1,985ft (600m) wide, and on the eastern section there is a huge bridge over the Amur river near Khabarovsk.

An English traveller produced a detailed description of the journey as it was in 1913, when the service started from the Yaroslav station in Moscow. The train, hauled by a finely maintained Pacific-type locomotive, comprised long cars in green-and-gold livery. In the passenger part of the train the corridors were fully carpeted, and the dining car had an ivory-white ceiling and panelled walls with large windows. The service also included a bathroom car, a pharmacy, and a car with reading and games rooms. Standards declined in the period between World Wars I and II, after the tsarist regime had been replaced by that of the communists and Russia had become the Union of Soviet Socialist Republics.

LEFT: The Australian XPT eight-car high-speed diesel electric passenger train was developed in 1981 as the Australian version of the British HST 125 (High Speed Train) by New South Wales Railways.

BELOW LEFT: The Sunlander *on the run from Brisbane to Cairns on Queensland Government Railways, Australia.*

OPPOSITE: An Australian W-class locomotive, now preserved. In the 1950s, this class of locomotive hauled the Broken Hill Express, *whose passenger services were eventually taken over by the famous* Indian-Pacific *service.*

The main element of the passenger services along the Trans-Siberian Railway was then provided by the *Trans-Siberian Express*, which had a special sleeping car and dining facilities. There was also the *Blue Express*, which included 'hard' and 'soft' accommodation as well as a sleeping car. These trains, which were relatively light with only eight or nine cars, took just under 10 days to complete the 5,973-mile (9612-km) journey from Moscow to Vladivostok at an average speed of a mere 25mph (40km/h). The situation improved little in the later period of the communist state between the end of World War II and the collapse of the U.S.S.R. into the Commonwealth of Independent States in 1990. In this later period, the service included four-bunk 'soft'-class compartments that were spacious and clean, but there was also a public-address system that spouted a constant stream of communist propaganda. The quality of everything, large and small, was decidedly poor. The electric locomotive and cars were of Czechoslovak and East German manufacture respectively, and it would not be unfair to say that virtually the only 'all-Russian' element of the service was the constant supply of tea from old-fashioned samovars.

Not that far from Vladivostok in global terms lies Japan. Here, just after its defeat in World War II, the Japanese authorities planned the construction of a straight railroad line linking Tokyo and Osaka by means of trains travelling at 125mph (200km/h). Given the massive extent of the reconstruction effort that had to be undertaken in the aftermath of the war, however, this initial plan failed to reach fruition and it was 1958 before an aerial survey of the planned route was made. Then, in the next year and within a week of parliamentary authorization for the plan, work on the line began with a ceremonial ground-breaking event. Only 65 months later, during 1965, the two cities were linked by their first full service.

Given the fact that a high-speed journey was the line's *raison d'être*, the alignment of the track was arranged so that every curve had a radius of at least 1.5miles (2.4km) and, with a view to avoiding urban congestion and minimizing noise, the line was in places supported at a height of 21ft (6.4m) on viaducts with high parapet walls.

Other aspects of the line were the lack of level crossings and the traverses of estuaries and river valleys on long viaducts. Some 66 tunnels, 12 of them more than 1.25miles (2km) long, were bored through the rock of mountains that stood in the track's path, and to mitigate the suction effect that can be created by two trains passing each other in opposite directions at high speed, in this instance at a combined velocity of more than 250mph (400km/h), the gap between the nearer rails of the opposing tracks in the tunnels was increased from the standard figure of 6ft 0in (1.8m) to a figure between 9ft 0in (2.74m) and 9ft 6in (2.89m). Because of the train service's high speed, care also had to be taken when building the embankments to ensure that there was an adequate degree of compactness in the heaped earth.

On every day in the time frame between 6.00 a.m. and 9.00 p.m., a Hikari (lightning) train leaves Tokyo every 15 minutes and covers the 322 miles (518km) to Osaka in the time of 3 hours 10 minutes, in the process stopping only at Nagoya and Kyoto, at an average speed of over 100mph (160km/h). Each train consists of 16 cars and carries an average of 1,000 passengers. Because of the tunnels and the cars' high windows, travellers do not get a chance to see much of the beautiful scenery through which the train progresses. It is only when the line crosses river valleys that they can appreciate the Japanese countryside and distant mountains, including Mount Fuji, of which there are superb views.

Today the Tokyo–Osaka route is the

busiest of several Shinkansen (bullet train) services, with trains departing Tokyo as often as every six minutes at peak travel times. West of Osaka, the Shinkansen network has been extended to Kobe, Okayama, Hiroshima and, by way of an undersea tunnel, to Hakata on the island of Kyushu. North of Tokyo, the Shinkansen system has been expanded to include Niigata, Yamagata, Sendai and Morioka on separate routes. Tokyo is thus the hub of a series of radiating lines, but there are no through trains between the western and eastern Shinkansen lines. However, there are regular express trains from Tokyo all

the way to Hakata on the Osaka line.

Service is provided by three classes of trains: the Kodama local trains that make frequent stops, the Hikari limited-express trains, and the Nozomi extra-fare super-express trains. On the section of the network between Tokyo and Osaka three generations of equipment are now in service, the newest dating from the early 1990s. The latest equipment is used for the Nozomi service, and during March 1997 the Nozomi 500 entered service between Osaka and Hakata. This unmistakable train regularly operates at up to 186mph (300km/h) and is now the fastest regularly

scheduled train in the world. North of Tokyo, there is a mixture of new train types in service, including the double-deck 'Max' trains.

During the 1960s, far to the south of Japan on the island continent of Australia, there were two trains running on entirely different routes but sharing the name *Brisbane Express*. One of these routes, intended mainly for business passengers, generally in a rush and with limited interest in the world outside the train, was that routed over the newer 643-mile (1035-km) coastal track, and much of this trip was run during the night. This service was actually

divided into two, the *Brisbane Limited Express* covering the distance in 15 hours 30 minutes and the slower *Brisbane Express* following in the time of 17 hours 50 minutes.

The other route was intended more for the tourist, and therefore offered considerably greater attractions and, while including a section covered at night, traversed most of the most pleasant country by day. A departure at 1.55 p.m. meant that the descent of the Cowan Bank and the crossing of the Hawkesbury river were made in good light, as was the run along the shores of Brisbane Waters. The passengers also had good views of the well-inhabited country as far as Wyong, and then of hillier and more timbered terrain nearly as far as Broadmeadow, which was the junction for trains to Newcastle. This was an area containing many coal mines, and much coal traffic could be seen on the way to Maitland, where the shorter coastal route branched off to the north. The 'main' route continued westward through a comparatively flat dairy-farming region as far as Singleton, which was passed at about nightfall. The line then began gradually to climb into the foothills of the Great Dividing Range via Murrurundi, the depot town for the banking engines required to assist the heavy traffic crossing the range in both directions, which included 1/40 gradients on both sides of the central Ardglen tunnel.

West of the Great Dividing Range, the line descended easily to Tamworth before ascending once more up the Moonbi Range to reach the Northern Tablelands. Daylight

ABOVE: *South Australian Railway's 3ft 6-inch Class 400 4-8-2 and 2-8-4 No. 407 leaving Port Pirie for Peterborough, originally Petersburg. Though here hauling freight, Garratt locomotives were used on the* Broken Hill Express *passenger service for many years.*

LEFT: *Locomotive No. N457 on the Melbourne– Albury* Twin City Express. *Albury, historically, was where passengers travelling between Sydney and Melbourne changed trains, swapping the standard gauge of the New South Wales Railway for the broad gauge of Victorian Railways.*

OPPOSITE: *No. R707, a 4-6-4 express passenger locomotive, used to haul broad-gauge (5ft 3in) passenger trains in Australia.*

reached the train as it was passing through the undulating countryside before Tenterfield, which was the last major town to be passed before the train crossed into Queensland, where there was a change-of-gauge station at Wallangarra, where the passengers had to transfer themselves and their possessions onto the narrow-gauge express to Brisbane through pleasant hilly country to the Darling Downs, which are some of the finest farming lands in Australia. Some 5 hours 30 minutes after leaving Wallangarra, the train reached the Toowoomba, famous for its magnificent gardens. The descent of the mountains from Toowoomba was beautiful but slow. As a result, the Queensland Government Railways introduced a co-ordinated bus/rail service between Toowoomba and Helidon, the latter located at the bottom of the range: travellers heading for Brisbane could therefore spend more than one hour in Toowoomba, and could then board the bus and rejoin the train at Helidon for the final run into Brisbane. In the reverse direction, inhabitants of Toowoomba could get home an hour ahead of the train by using the bus. The arrival of the *Brisbane Express* in Brisbane was shortly after dusk at 6.25 p.m., some 28 hours 30 minutes after the service's departure from Sydney and after a run of 715 miles (1150km).

This great service no longer operates, however, as it was cancelled after a great length of the line from Glen Innes to the Queensland border had been abandoned.

There can have been few areas more disheartening to earlier generations of

Australians than the region spanning the border of South Australia and New South Wales. By 1876, however, lead sulphide (the ore from which lead and, to a lesser extent, gold are extracted) was found on the New South Wales side of the border, and by 1883 the Silverton area was booming with mines and even smelters. In the same year, lead sulphide was discovered at Broken Hill and the government of South Australia, appreciating the commercial importance of the region, hastily built a narrow-gauge line from Petersburg (now Peterborough) to the border. The line was completed in January 1887, but the government of New South Wales refused to allow the line to be extended across the border. This situation resulted in the establishment of a private

company to create and run the Silverton Tramway Company as a link between the South Australian Railway's line and Broken Hill via Silverton. By this time Silverton, a town with 36 hotels, was already in decline, while Broken Hill was still a boom town and, though now declining, remained so through most of the 20th century.

Although it is geographically in New South Wales, Broken Hill uses the South Australian time zone, and most of its commercial business is undertaken with Adelaide, which is altogether closer than Sydney. To make this connection with Adelaide, a regular train service connected the two cities, the *Broken Hill Express* being one of the few Australian passenger express services hauled for many years by

Garratt locomotives. The service was basically of the overnight type, and the South Australian Railway built up the tonnage with freight wagons. To the east of the border, the Silverton Tramway Company, with its 36 miles (58km) of line, provided the locomotives and a number of the freight cars. The locomotives originally employed to haul the service were of the 'Colonial Mogul' type, followed in 1912 by 'A'-class 4-6-0 locomotives, in 1951 by 'W'-class 4-8-2 semi-streamlined locomotives similar to those used in Western Australia, and from 1960 by Co-Co diesel-electric locomotives up to 1970, when the standard-gauge system bypassed the private line.

Early traffic on the South Australian Railway side was handled by 'Y' or 'X'-class examples of the Colonial Mogul type of locomotive, but the growth of traffic soon required that larger locomotives be adopted and this led to the design of the highly successful 'T' class of 4-8-0 locomotives, of which 78 examples were built from 1903 onward with some units remaining in service right to the end of the steam era. These locomotives hauled the services 140 miles (225km) to Terowie, where there was a change to the broad-gauge system, with an 'S'-class 4-4-0 locomotive taking over for the additional 140 miles (225km) to Adelaide. The 'S'-class units were replaced in the 1920s by larger and more powerful engines. In 1953, the '400'-class Garratt locomotives were introduced and rapidly took over the Broken Hill traffic, and from 1959 the

South Australian Railway bought '830'-class Co-Co diesel-electric locomotives that then took over from steam locomotives on this semi-desert route. This standardization rang the death knell for the *Broken Hill Express*, for the *Indian-Pacific* eventually took over the passenger traffic on the line and the broad-gauge services were withdrawn from Terowie.

In the 1950s, the *Broken Hill Express* left Broken Hill at 7.48 p.m. behind a Silverton W-class locomotive, covering what was possibly the most scenic part of this semi-desert journey in darkness to the border, which it reached at 9.21 p.m. Here a 400-class Garratt locomotive took over for the run to Peterborough, where passengers for Port Pirie had to change at 3.58 a.m. The train reversed out of Peterborough, with a new locomotive for the short run to Terowie, where Adelaide passengers changed to the broad-gauge service at 4.50 a.m. After a 20-minute refreshment pause, the broad-gauge service departed for its 9.20 a.m. arrival in Adelaide after a journey of 362 miles (582km).

Although a rapidly escalating level of railroad construction was evident in Australia from the 1850s, it was not until 1917 that a passenger could travel across the continent between the Pacific and Indian Oceans, a railroad distance then reckoned at 2,704 miles (4352km). When this passage finally became possible, Australia still operated a number of different railway gauges, and this made the journey a considerable effort as there were many changes involved and the route, now

OPPOSITE: The last day of Australian
Steam fortnight. No. 3801 at Barry Road
Bridge en route from Melbourne to Albury,
and then to Sydney

RIGHT: NSW No. 8176 nearing
Broadmeadows with the overnight
Melbourne Express *from Sydney.*

fairly direct and by standard-gauge track
throughout, at that time meandered by way
of Melbourne and Adelaide.

In its early days, the transcontinental
service demanded that the traveller boarded
the standard-gauge train in Sydney in time
for a departure at 7.25 p.m. and a night run
to the Victorian border at Albury, where at
7.23 a.m. there was 23 minutes for the
passenger to change onto the broad-gauge
train that reached Melbourne at 12.51 p.m.
Here there was a gap of some 3 hours 30

minutes, allowing the passenger time for a
meal and other refreshment before he
boarded the broad-gauge train that departed
Melbourne at 4.30 p.m. for an overnight
passage to Adelaide in South Australia,
reached at 9.55 a.m. on the second day.
Some 50 minutes later, the passenger was
on yet another broad-gauge train north to
Terowie, where 30 minutes were available
for refreshments and the change to another
narrow-gauge train that circumnavigated its
way to Port Augusta, reached at 10.05 p.m.

on the second day for yet another change,
in this instance to a standard-gauge train for
the journey across the Nullarbor Plain.

The crossing of this vast region of
semi-desert then took about one and a half
days, and this section included the world's
longest railroad 'straight' of 297 miles
(478km). The first halt on the western side
of the Nullarbor Plain was the gold-mining
town of Kalgoorlie, reached at 1.38 p.m. on
the fourth day of the trip. At Kalgoorlie the
passenger had to wait until 5.15 p.m. before

he could leave on the narrow-gauge express
service to Perth, which the train reached at
9.47 a.m. on the morning of the fifth day.
The whole journey had taken just over four-
and-a-half days, allowing for the two-hour
time difference between the western and
eastern sides of the continent.

It was not until 1969 that the route via
Broken Hill to Perth was completely
revised to a standard-gauge track
arrangement, and in 1970 the *Indian-Pacific*
service was inaugurated, cutting the journey

of 2,461 miles (3961km) to a time of just over two-and-a-half days. Since then, a standard-gauge line has been laid almost into Adelaide. Unlike European railway systems, which would provide a through-car service, for the section between Melbourne and Port Pirie via Adelaide, the *Indian-Pacific* takes a lengthy and time-consuming side jaunt from near Crystal Brook to Keswick in the Adelaide suburbs and back.

The *Indian-Pacific* now departs Sydney at 2.55 p.m., soon passing through Sydney's inner suburbs, and reaches the open railroad at Blacktown for acceleration to its highest cruising speed. The train crosses the Hawkesbury river beyond Penrith, and then starts the climb into the Blue Mountains: the current route is the third ascent, and provides excellent views of these superb mountains, with similar views possible on the descent along the western sides of the range. At the foot of the mountains the train moves through rolling farming country to Parkes, which is reached after nightfall. From Parkes, the route covers virtually nothing but semi-desert country almost the entire remaining distance to Perth.

On the other side of the Tasman Sea from Australia lies New Zealand. The nation's most important commercial centre is Wellington, on the North Island, and in earlier times this was linked to the city of Christchurch, the seat of provincial government and main gateway to the vast farming hinterland of Canterbury on the South Island, by coastal steamers. The first proposal for a rail line to connect the two cities was suggested as early as 1861, but it

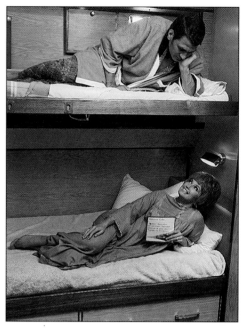

was only 11 years later, in 1872, that work began on a broad-gauge line north from Christchurch, this being altered to the 3ft 6in (1.07m) gauge in 1877. A line south from Picton, the port opposite Wellington on the north-east corner of the South Island, was started in 1875. Progress was then made as and when the political will and economic resources allowed, but by 1916 the northern line had reached Wharanui, only 56 miles (90km) from Picton, while the southern section had reached Parnassus, only 83 miles (133km) from Christchurch. It was to be another 20 years before further real progress was made toward closing the gap through the mountainous terrain around Kaikoura, and the complete 216-mile (348-km) line opened only in December 1945.

In 1954 the introduction of a roll-

RIGHT: *The Rotorua-Auckland express, headed by a K-class 4-8-4 locomotive No. 909 at Eureka, between Morrinsville and Hamilton. The Rotorua-bound train in the background is leaving the crossing loop.*

BELOW RIGHT: *The* Endeavour *express running daily between Wellington and Napier on New Zealand's North Island. The train is headed by a 1,063kW Da-class A1A-A1A diesel-electric locomotive and comprises day coaches and a licensed buffet-car.*

OPPOSITE
ABOVE LEFT: *The first* Indian-Pacific *express leaves Perth, Western Australia, on its trip eastwards across the continent on 30 August 1970.*

ABOVE RIGHT: *First-class honeymoon suite aboard the Australian trans-continental* Indian-Pacific *express.*

BELOW LEFT: *The* Silver Star *express, headed by a 2,051kW Dx-class Co-Co diesel-electric locomotive. It ran overnight, Sunday through Friday, between Auckland and Wellington in New Zealand's North Island.*

ABOVE: *The 'Grass Grub', the local nickname for the Picton–Christchurch train, in Kaikoura station with No. DF6064 in charge. The Kaikoura mountains and the Pacific Ocean are in the background.*

LEFT: *Interior of the buffet car of the* Southerner.

OPPOSITE: *The southbound* Southerner *is hauled across Otago Harbour on a causeway. A small country with limited population, New Zealand nevertheless had its share of crack passenger services.*

on/roll-off rail ferry altered the connecting sea crossing from Wellington, and in 1988 the service was further improved with rebuilt rolling stock. The journey from Wellington to Christchurch has several interesting aspects. The 50-mile (80-km) sea crossing can be very memorable, especially in the event of adverse weather in the Cook Strait before the ship reaches the more sheltered waters of Marlborough Sound. Then there is the ride through the hills of Marlborough, followed by the exhilarating passage through the harsher mountains around Kaikoura with the Pacific Ocean as an intimate companion, and finally the gentler landscape leading toward the Canterbury Plains.

The concept of a luxury service for the *Coastal Pacific Express* on the route linking Picton and Christchurch followed the successful introduction of such a service between Christchurch and Greymouth through the alpine scenery of the South Island. Several of the cars were converted with larger windows, separated by narrow pillars for excellent fields of view. The high-backed seats are fitted with sheepskin covers. Other aspects of the accommodation include full carpeting, large ventilators and window curtains. The livery is a combination of interior pink-and-grey and exterior mid-blue with red-and-white bands.

With all the passengers embarked, the train cruises out of Picton (originally known as Waitohi) and completes a steep climb before traversing the Waitohi viaduct. By the time the train has reached Elevation, only 2.5 miles (4km) from Picton, the

mountains have taken on an alpine aspect, with stands of conifers and logging tracks, but the pastures visible below with their scattered trees are more similar in appearance to English parkland. Before Blenheim, the train passes over the Wairau river on a long but low bridge. Blenheim itself serves as the gateway to the increasingly well-known wine-growing regions of Marlborough, and past this town the train starts another long ascent, in this instance toward the bleaker regions around the Dashwood Pass. Another gradient takes the train to the unusual bridge over the Awatere river: this is a combination bridge with the railway carried on an upper deck with the road on the deck below it. After passing over the Blind river, the train then travels along a long causeway to get across the large salt lakes on the approaches to Lake Grasmere. Near Wharanui, the train starts on a long section of coastal running, and here the passengers can enjoy about 90 minutes of magnificent scenery before the stop at Kaikoura. For much of the way, the railway and the road are squeezed into a narrow strip between the mountains on the west and the shore on the east. In about 62 miles (100km) of line to Oaro there are 20 tunnels, several embankments and steep cuttings, sharp curves and isolated bridges.

The line's winding alignment, which follows the ins-and-outs of the coastline, ends on the approach to Kaikoura. This is a fishing port and former whaling station, and lies on a peninsula about mid-way between Picton and Christchurch. The train pauses briefly here before resuming its journey by

means of another curving viaduct, then there is another stretch of spectacular coastal running along a section of line marked by nine tunnels. Beyond Oaro, at sea level again, the train climbs steeply and passes through the Amuri Bluff tunnel and then the Okarahia viaduct. Soon the suburbs of Christchurch come into view and the journey is complete as the train pulls into the station.

LEFT: The northbound Southerner *stands in Dunedin station with DJ-class locomotives 3211 and 3050 in charge.*

Picture Acknowledgements
*Amtrak: pages 10, 11 below, 21
*Berne-Lötschberg-Simplon: page 34 above left
*British Columbia Railways: pages 6, 7
*British Rail: page 52 above
*Canadian National Railway: page 9 all
*Canadian Pacific Railway: page 8
*Great Northern Railway: page 13 above
Military Archives & Research Services, Lincolnshire, England: pages 11, above left and right, 32, 50 both, 51 both
*Milwaukee Road: page 12 above
*New Zealand Railways: pages 58 below, 59 both
*Queensland Government Railways: page 52 below
©Railfotos, Millbrook House Limited, Oldbury, W. Midlands, England: Title pages, pages 4, 5, 12 below, 13 below, 14 all, 15 both, 16, 17, 18, 19 both, 20 both, 22, 23 both, 24, 25, 26, 27 all, 28, 29 both, 30 both, 31 both, 33, 36, 37, 39 right, 40, 42, 47, 48, 53, 54 both, 55, 56, 57, 60, 61 both, 62–63
*SNCF: pages 34 above and below right, 35, 38, 39 left, 41 both
*South African Railways: page 43 all, 44, 45, 46 both
*Swiss Federal Railways: page 34 below left
*Western Australia Government Railways: page 58 above left and right

*Print/transparency through **Military Archives & Research Services, Lincolnshire, England.**